Holiday Parties

Let's Throw a

Thanksgiving Party!

Rachel Lynette

PowerKiDS press.

New York

For my family

Published in 2012 by The Rosen Publishing Group, Inc.
29 East 21st Street, New York, NY 10010

First Edition

Editor: Joanne Randolph
Layout Design: Greg Tucker

Photo Credits: Cover, p. 10 (top) © www.iStockphoto.com/Sean Locke; pp. 4–5 Ariel Skelley/Getty Images; pp. 6–7 SuperStock/Getty Images; pp. 8, 11, 14 (bottom), 15 Shutterstock.com; p. 9 Library of Congress/ digital version by Science Faction/Getty Images; p. 10 (bottom) Comstock Images/Getty Images; p. 14 (top) Foodcollection/Getty Images; p. 16 iStockphoto/Thinkstock; p. 18 Gary John Norman/Getty Images; p. 19 Brooklyn Productions/Getty Images; p. 21 Thinkstock Images/Comstock/Thinkstock; p. 22 Jupiterimages/Creatas/Thinkstock.

Library of Congress Cataloging-in-Publication Data

Lynette, Rachel.
 Let's throw a Thanksgiving party! / by Rachel Lynette. — 1st ed.
    p. cm. — (Holiday parties)
 Includes index.
 ISBN 978-1-4488-2573-8 (library binding) — ISBN 978-1-4488-2735-0 (pbk.) —
 ISBN 978-1-4488-2736-7 (6-pack)
 1. Thanksgiving decorations—Juvenile literature. 2. Thanksgiving cooking—Juvenile literature.
 3. Thanksgiving Day—Juvenile literature. 4. Children's parties—Juvenile literature. I. Title.
 TT900.T5L96 2012
 745.594'1649—dc22
                                                  2010034278

Manufactured in the United States of America

CPSIA Compliance Information: Batch #WW11PK: For Further Information contact Rosen Publishing, New York, New York at 1-800-237-9932

Contents

A Time of Thanks

What do you think about when you think of Thanksgiving? Maybe you think about a big Thanksgiving dinner with turkey, mashed potatoes, and pumpkin pie for dessert. Maybe you think about spending time with your family and your friends. Maybe you think

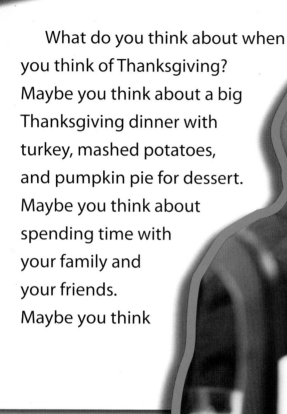

Turkey is commonly served at Thanksgiving dinner. Families come together to give thanks for each other and the other good things in their lives.

about all the things for which you are thankful.

You will likely eat Thanksgiving dinner with your family. However, you may also want to have a Thanksgiving party for your friends. This book will give you ideas for food, games, and other party **activities**. Throwing a Thanksgiving party is a great way to **celebrate** the holiday!

The First Thanksgiving

In the winter of 1620, the **Pilgrims** landed at Plymouth Rock, in Massachusetts. They sailed there from England on a ship called the *Mayflower*. The Pilgrims did not know how to find food in this new land. They did not know how to plant crops. Luckily, a **Native American** named

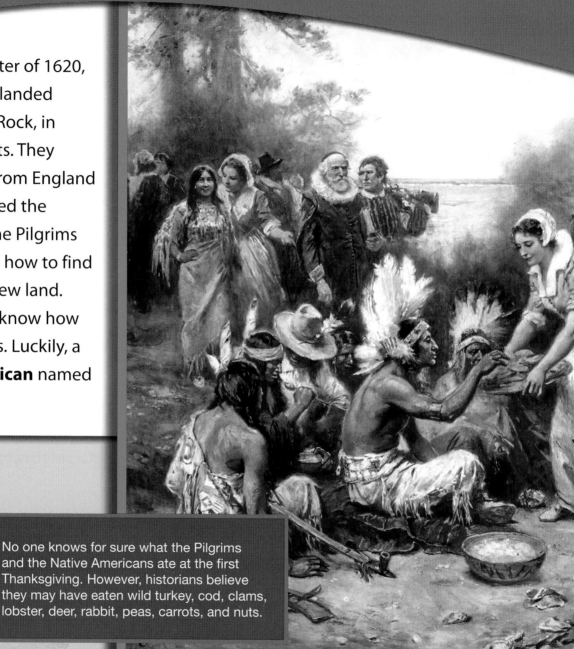

No one knows for sure what the Pilgrims and the Native Americans ate at the first Thanksgiving. However, historians believe they may have eaten wild turkey, cod, clams, lobster, deer, rabbit, peas, carrots, and nuts.

Tisquantum, or Squanto, helped them. He taught the Pilgrims which plants were **edible**. He taught them to hunt and how to plant corn and other crops.

By the fall of 1621, the Pilgrims had enough food to store for winter. They held a big **feast** to celebrate the harvest. They **invited** the Native Americans to celebrate with them. That was the very first Thanksgiving!

Get Ready!

You will want to start planning your party at the beginning of November. Make a list of the guests you want to invite. Most people spend Thanksgiving with their families, so you may want to throw your party before or after Thanksgiving Day.

You will want to make a list of everything you will need for your party. What kind of

Lists make it easier to remember things. For your party, you will want to make a list of the things you need to do, a list of supplies you need, and a list of guests to invite.

People used to celebrate Thanksgiving on different dates. Then, in 1863, President Abraham Lincoln, shown here, made Thanksgiving a national holiday. He said that it would be celebrated on the last Thursday of November. It is now celebrated on the fourth Thursday of November.

decorations will you make or buy? What supplies will you need? Decide what kind of food you want to serve, and make a shopping list. Do not forget to think about what you will need for games and other activities. You may want to ask an adult to help you plan your party.

Decoration Fun

What can you do to decorate for your party? Fall colors such as yellow, orange, red, and brown are often used at Thanksgiving time. You can make paper cutouts of turkeys, pumpkins, corn on the cob, fall leaves, and Pilgrim hats. You could draw pictures of Pilgrims and Native

Left: Pumpkins and other gourds make great fall decorations. Hay, fall leaves, and cranberries are good Thanksgiving decorations, too! *Top:* To make a turkey, as this girl has done, trace your hand on a piece of paper. Make the thumb into the head of your turkey and use the fingers for the feathers. You could also cut out feathers from colored paper and glue them to your hand shape.

Pinecones and leaves turn this turkey cookie into a fun table decoration. To make a cookie like this, make turkey-shaped sugar cookies and press candy corns into the tail.

Americans. You could also make a sign that says "Happy Thanksgiving!" to hang on the wall or over a fireplace.

You can use natural things to decorate, too. You could make a Thanksgiving wreath from colorful leaves. You could place small pumpkins and **gourds** on tables and in the windowsills. Pinecones and Indian corn, or maize, make good decorations, too.

Make a Pinecone Turkey Centerpiece

Here is a fun project that will make a great centerpiece for your Thanksgiving table.

What you need:

A large, roundish pinecone
Yellow, black, red, and
      orange paper
2 small googly eyes
White glue
Scissors
Stickers

What you do:

1

Cut out a head for your turkey. A simple oval shape will work well.

2

Glue on the googly eyes.

3

Cut a small yellow triangle for the beak and a long red shape for the wattle that hangs down from a turkey's neck. Glue them to the head, as shown.

4

Glue the head onto the front of the narrow end of the pinecone.

5

Cut out about 10–15 feather shapes from different-colored construction paper. Glue them to the back of the pinecone to make the turkey's feathers. If you want, you can use real feathers instead of paper ones. Most craft stores sell colorful feathers in bags.

6

If you are having trouble getting your pinecone to stand up, use a large, upside-down paper cup as a stand for your turkey. You can decorate the cup with paper or stickers.

There are many things you can do to make your table special. An orange, yellow, or leaf-covered tablecloth will make your table look like it is ready for a feast. You can make Thanksgiving napkin rings with pipe cleaners and plastic beads, too. Just thread yellow, orange, and red beads onto a colored pipe cleaner. Then bend the pipe cleaner around your napkins.

Pick fall colors for your table, such as red, gold, and brown. Apples, pinecones, and small pumpkins will add to the harvesttime look!

This colorful corn is called maize, or Indian corn. It can make a great centerpiece for your table.

You could have guests make fun Thanksgiving place mats when they first get to your house. Give each guest a thick rectangle of paper and an uncooked corncob. Guests can roll their corncobs in a tray of red, orange, or yellow paint. Then they can roll the cob on their paper to make a fun print!

Tasty Thanksgiving Treats

You do not have to make a whole Thanksgiving dinner for your guests, but you will want to have some fun Thanksgiving treats. Give your guests turkey footprints by spreading cream cheese on round crackers. Then place chow mien noodles on each cookie to look like a turkey footprint!

Try This!

1. Mix a few spoonfuls of whole-berry cranberry sauce with soft cream cheese. Spread the mix on a flour tortilla.
2. Put one to two slices of turkey on the tortilla.
3. Roll up the tortilla and put four or five toothpicks in it.
4. Slice between the toothpicks.

Pilgrim hat treats

You can also make yummy Pilgrim hats. Just use white frosting to stick a miniature peanut butter cup to the back of a fudge-striped cookie. The frosting is the hatband, so make sure it shows around the edges.

Do not forget to give your guests something good to drink. Quench their thirst with apple cider or cranberry punch.

Time for Games!

The first Thanksgiving lasted for three days. During that time, the Pilgrims and the Native Americans played games and ran races. Playing games at your party is a great way to celebrate Thanksgiving! The Pilgrims ate

Divide your guests into two teams. Set a timer for 2 minutes. Whichever team husks the most corn in that time wins!

Many families enjoy playing football on Thanksgiving. You could try to play flag or touch football at your party, too.

walnuts, chestnuts, and acorns. Hide these kinds of nuts in their shells. Then let your guests search for them.

Your guests may enjoy playing a **traditional** harvesttime game, too. Have a corn-husking contest! Husking corn means removing the green covering and the silk, or hairlike parts, from the corn. Corn husking can be messy, so you might want to play this game outside.

Tree of Thanks

CANDY!

my best friend David

my teacher Miss Hall

my dog Buster

Summer vacation!

my sister Jane

MY MOM

no homework

What are you thankful for? It is important to think about the things you are thankful for on Thanksgiving. One way to help your guests think about what they are thankful for is to make a tree of thanks.

Use brown butcher paper to make a tree trunk and branches.

Even if you do not make a tree of thanks for your party, you could make one with your family. It is a great way to remember all the good things in your lives.

Put the tree on the wall. Then your guests can cut leaves from yellow, orange, and red construction paper. Ask your guests to write what they are thankful for on the leaves. Then they can tape or glue the leaves to the tree. Soon you will have a beautiful tree that is full of thanks!

You may want to cut out leaves ahead of time for your guests to use on the tree of thanks. If you explain the project at the beginning of the party, your guests can add leaves whenever they think of something for which they are thankful.

Do Something Good

It is good to be thankful for what you have. It is also important to remember that not everyone has enough money to have a big feast at Thanksgiving. Thanksgiving is a time when you can help some of those people.

One thing you can do is have each of your guests bring canned food to your party. Then you can **donate** the food to a food bank. Food banks give food to people in need.

You could also **volunteer** to do some work for a **charity**. Ask an adult to help you find a charity that allows children to volunteer. Helping others will make you feel good, too!

Helping others is a good way to remember how the Native Americans helped the Pilgrims. Many historians think that the Pilgrims would have died if Squanto had not helped them.

Glossary

activities (ak-TIH-vuh-teez) Actions or things to do.

celebrate (SEH-luh-brayt) To honor an important moment by doing things.

charity (CHER-uh-tee) A group that gives help to the needy.

decorations (deh-kuh-RAY-shunz) Objects that make things prettier.

donate (DOH-nayt) To give something away.

edible (EH-deh-bul) Fit to be eaten.

feast (FEEST) A large meal.

gourds (GORDZ) Round fruits from vines, whose hard shells are used to make bowls.

invited (in-VYT-ed) Asked people if they will come to a party.

Native American (NAY-tiv uh-MER-uh-kun) A person who lived in America before the Europeans came. A Native American is sometimes called an American Indian.

Pilgrims (PIL-grumz) The people who sailed on the *Mayflower* in 1620 from England to America in search of freedom to practice their own beliefs.

traditional (truh-DIH-shuh-nul) Done in a way that has been passed down over time.

volunteer (vah-lun-TEER) To give one's time without pay.

Index

Web Sites

Due to the changing nature of Internet links, PowerKids Press has developed an online list of Web sites related to the subject of this book. This site is updated regularly. Please use this link to access the list:
www.powerkidslinks.com/hp/thanks/